Tell Us More About Maine, Grandpa!

Written By Ed Linz

Tell Us More About Maine, Grandpa
Copyright © 2025 by Ed Linz All rights reserved
First Edition: 2025

Paperback ISBN: 978-1-7367348-8-9
eBook ISBN: 979-1-7367348-9-6

This story is intended as a work of fiction. Any resemblance of the characters contained herein to persons living or dead, is purely coincidental.

All rights reserved. No part of this publication may be reproduced or transmitted in any form or by any means, electronic or mechanical, including photocopy, recording or any information storage or retrieval system now known or to be invented without written permission from the author, except by a reviewer who wishes to quote brief passages in connection with a review written for inclusion in a magazine, newspaper, broadcast, blog, or online.

TABLE OF CONTENTS

Background	1
Northern Lights	2
Lake in Winter	4
Blue Lobsters	6
Forest Land	8
Seaplane	10
The 20th of Maine	12
Mount Katahdin	14
Geothermal Heat	16
Benedict Arnold	18
Black Flies	20
Lighthouses	22
Thoreau-Wabanaki Trail	24
Aquaculture	26
Moose	28
First People to Live in Maine	30
Coldwater fish	32
Bears	34
Lost on a Mountain	36
Fire Towers	38
Mills	40
Maine Coon Cats	42
Author's Note	44

This book is dedicated to my wife, Sharry, who introduced me to Maine, and our wonderful Maine neighbors, especially Lynn and Betty

BACKGROUND

Art Linkletter, a radio personality during the 1940's, included a segment on his shows called "*Kids Say the Darndest Things.*" In its original format, Linkletter would pose a question to a child who would answer with what would be an entirely innocent, but often comedic, response. It quickly became a popular feature and was continued on Linkletter's television series from the early 1950's to 1969 in front of a live audience.

As a grandparent and classroom teacher, I have found that children also "*Ask The Darndest Questions.*" Often these questions are about things that they see daily, namely their communities and home state. With that in mind, it seems appropriate to answer some of those typical questions about Maine. Several pages could be devoted to providing complete answers to each of the questions, but my intent has been to provide as much interesting information as possible within space limits. I encourage all readers, children and adults, to engage in further discussion and do research on these and other aspects of our wonderful, fascinating state of Maine.

I want to thank all of our friends throughout Maine for suggesting topics and providing encouragement. I am particularly grateful to our local librarians, Jessica, Andrea, Mary, and PJ, at the Shaw Public Library in Greenville, Lisa, the owner of our local bookstore, and Lynn, Betty, Bob, and Peggy Joy. Also, this book would not have been possible without the assistance of our family caregiver, Rose, who has provided invaluable health care for our family while I have been researching and writing.

GRAMPS, SOMETIMES I HAVE SEEN PURPLE, PINK, AND GREEN COLORS IN OUR MAINE SKY AT NIGHT. WHAT IS THIS?

WHAT YOU ARE SEEING, BETTY, is due to charged particles (mainly electrons and protons) which have been expelled by the sun. As they approach Earth, these particles are drawn to Earth's magnetic North and South poles and enter our atmosphere at very high speeds. As they collide with molecules of gas in Earth's atmosphere, the gases emit light at different colors, primarily green, but also, in lesser amounts, red, blue, purple, yellow, and pink. The colors we see depend on whether the gas molecules are oxygen or nitrogen or a mix of the two and how high up in our atmosphere the collisions take place.

These colorful lights which can often be seen in the northern regions of the northern hemisphere are usually called "The Northern Lights." Their formal name in Latin is, "Aurora Borealis." In the southern hemisphere, they are called "Aurora Australis" or "The Southern Lights." Astronomers watching the sun can predict when there is a good chance of seeing an aurora. There are websites which make daily predictions when and where to look.

Our sun is very active. It is constantly having nuclear fusion explosions creating heat and light. This light travels the 93 million miles to Earth at 186,000 miles each second, arriving about 8-9 minutes later. These explosions on the sun also shoot out large amounts of charged particles in what is called the "solar wind." This "wind" (which creates the Auroras) doesn't reach Earth for 2-4 days. This allows astronomers to send out a warning if a potentially harmful solar event has occurred which can damage electronic equipment here on Earth.

HEY, POPPOP, IN WINTER HERE IN MAINE OUR LAKE NEVER FREEZES SOLID. IT JUST GETS MAYBE A FOOT OF ICE ON IT, WHICH IS GOOD BECAUSE WE CAN DRILL A HOLE AND DO SOME ICE FISHING. BUT WHY DOESN'T IT FREEZE SOLID?

Water is fascinating, Charlie. Over half of the human body is water. Life on Earth would not be possible without it. And water is complicated – very complicated. It has three states: solid (ice), liquid (water), and gas (steam) depending on the temperature and pressure around it. But even in its liquid state, water has different properties at varying temperatures.

At the atmospheric pressure found at sea level, water boils at 212° F and freezes at 32° F. When water cools below 212° F, it becomes denser (heavier). When our winter air temperatures decrease, the water at the surface of our lakes is colder than that below, becomes heavier and sinks. This process continues until most of the water temperature in the lake is about 40° F. At that temperature something almost magical happens: water stops becoming denser and now becomes lighter as the temperature approaches freezing!

As the water on the surface cools, it becomes lighter than the 40° F water below and "floats" on it. When the temperature of this surface water reaches 32° F and begins to freeze, it turns into a thin layer of ice which floats on the water below.

As this ice on top of the lake becomes thicker, it forms a protective barrier to keep the water below from being exposed to the cold air above, which keeps it from freezing. The thickness of this layer of ice will very slowly increase until we can walk on it, or even drive a vehicle on it safely, but the fish below will be just fine! Their only challenge is to not be tempted by your bait as you dangle it through a hole in the ice!

GRANDDADDY, ARE THERE REALLY BLUE LOBSTERS?

They're rare, Kate, but they do exist. A blue one shows up in about every two million lobsters – and it's a vibrant blue, almost the color of the metal cobalt. Almost all lobster shells have a mixture of various pigments (color) which are usually red, yellow, and blue. When these are mixed together, you end up with that typical greenish-brown color you see on most lobster shells. But when you cook a blue lobster, it turns red just like every other lobster in the pot.

Those odds I mentioned, one in two million, are an estimate. No one knows for certain, but every year several blue ones are hauled in by lobstermen in their traps. You may not have heard of this, but there are even rarer colors for lobsters, such as yellow, red, calico (orange and black) and even white. Another rare variation is a lobster which has brown on one side and orange on the other! It's not safe for a lobster to have these unusual colors because it makes it more difficult for them to hide from predators. The usual color pattern of greenish-brown acts as great camouflage while the lobster crawls around on rocky ocean bottoms. Perhaps more blue lobsters are born, but they're lost because they can be seen more easily by predators in the ocean.

Most Maine commercial lobstermen will not sell a blue lobster for eating, but instead donate them to an aquarium for scientific research. There have been reports, though, of people eating a blue lobster and finding that it tastes just the same as every other lobster. I'm not sure that I could eat one!

GRANDPA, TINA TOLD ME THAT MAINE HAS MORE FOREST LAND THAN ANY OTHER STATE. IS THAT REALLY TRUE?

That's certainly true, Ella! According to the U.S. Forest Service, there are over 17 million acres of forest land in Maine – by far, the highest percentage of forest cover than any other state. It's estimated that Maine has one billion live trees, located mostly in the northern counties. These numbers are obviously estimates, but they are "informed estimates" because crews count trees in only 3000 locations in our forests each year. Trees, of course, are living creatures which are in a continuous natural growth and death cycle. In addition to the trees which are harvested, others spring from seeds, some die, and some are destroyed by fire, weather events, and insects.

Forests are an important part of Maine's economy. Our trees provide 25,000 jobs to Mainers, who harvest or thin over 400,000 acres of forests each year. Different types of trees are used for differing purposes. Fir, spruce, and hemlock are generally designated for paper product production and structural lumber. Hardwoods like oak, maple, and birch are used for furniture and flooring. Some of our trees are processed in Canada and some here in Maine. You'll see lumber trucks going both directions.

One tree can have as many as 200,000 leaves on it – most of this is returned to the soil below as nutrients. One acre of trees can grow 4000 pounds of wood in a year while absorbing nearly 6000 pounds of carbon dioxide and producing over 4000 pounds of oxygen! And paper made from trees can be recycled 4-5 times before losing its strength. Our trees are truly magnificent – we're lucky to have so many here.

I SAW A SEAPLANE LAND IN ONE OF OUR NEARBY PONDS THE OTHER DAY. POPS, CAN I GO UP IN ONE SOMEDAY?

Seaplane

Floatplane

Old DC-3 aircraft converted to "World's Largest Floatplane"

FIRST OF ALL, PEGGY JOY, what you saw was a "floatplane" because it lands on floats attached to the bottom of the aircraft. A "seaplane" floats by itself on a floating hull (notice difference in photos). But most Mainers use the terms interchangeably. Many of our seaplanes here in Maine do take passengers on sightseeing tours. It can be expensive if you want to go on a long flight, but a short sightseeing ride in one of these planes can cost as little as $100 a person. I did this several years ago with your Mom, and it was great. We even saw several moose having lunch on some plants in a pond!

Because over 5000 lakes and ponds are scattered all around our state, there are several seaplane bases where pilots can get fuel and services to take passengers to these lakes. A large number of hunting and fishing lodges and campsites are located deep in Maine woods, so seaplanes are often the best way to reach them. There are publications, phone apps, and internet maps providing details of shorelines and rockpiles and other important facts for seaplane pilots planning flights to these remote locations. Although many of these lakes and ponds are on private property, you can still go because Maine law states that any pond over eight acres belongs to the people of Maine.

There is a very large seaplane with an interesting history in Greenville. In 1987, two local aviators got the idea of taking a very old DC-3 airplane they located in Texas and adding the only remaining floats from WW II to it. Once put together, their creation became "the world's largest floatplane." I was lucky enough to see its most recent flight in 2024.

GRAMPA, ONE OF MY BUDDIES WAS TALKING LAST WEEK ABOUT "THE 20TH OF MAINE." WHAT WAS THAT?

Colonel Chamberlain leading the 20th of Maine in a charge down a hill against Confederate troops at Little Round Top at the Battle of Gettysburg in the Civil War, July 2, 1863

Billy, I bet that when your friend was talking about the "20th of Maine," he also mentioned a "Colonel Chamberlain." Both are very famous due to heroic action in the Civil War fought from 1861-1865 between the northern and southern states.

Both sides had large armies of volunteers; the northern forces were called "The Union Army" and the southerners were "Confederates." The 20th Maine Volunteer Infantry Regiment was organized in 1862. Their unit, assigned to the Army of the Potomac, was in combat just a few months later during winter battles near Fredericksburg, Virginia. Union forces suffered dispiriting defeats under unimaginably harsh conditions with smallpox ravaging many troops. The following summer, Joshua L. Chamberlain, previously a Bowdoin college professor, was promoted to command the 20th. Within weeks, Chamberlain and his men were defending an important hill, Little Round Top, during the Battle of Gettysburg in Pennsylvania. It was a fierce battle involving hand-to-hand fighting. When the 20th began to run out of ammunition, the situation looked dire, but Colonel Chamberlain ordered "Fix Bayonets" and the surviving soldiers of the 20th charged down the hill overwhelming their opponents from Alabama. Many credit Maine's 20th with saving the Union Army at Gettysburg by their courageous actions.

The 20th went on to fight numerous other critical battles in Virginia and participated in the surrender ceremony at Appomattox Courthouse in May 1865. Of the original 1621 soldiers in the 20th, close to half were killed or wounded. All of these Mainers were truly heroes.

IS HIKING ON MOUNT KATAHDIN REALLY THAT DANGEROUS, POPPOP?

Mount Katahdin from Abol Stream

Hiking on the top of Katahdin

As you can see from these two photos, Philip, Katahdin looks beautiful from a distance, but when hiking it, there can be some serious, and even dangerous, challenges. Because it's the highest mountain in Maine at 5282 feet, the high altitude and its location sometimes generate situations where Katahdin actually creates its own weather. This happens when air blowing into the side of the mountain is directed upward into cooler air where moisture is less likely to evaporate. This moisture forms clouds and even rain or snow – even when the weather at the bottom of the mountain is warm and dry.

Courtesy of www.sectionhiker.com

Several years ago, your dad and I found ourselves in a very dangerous situation on top of Katahdin. When we began our hike in early August the weather was warm with a slight mist. But when we reached the summit, the temperature had fallen to the low 40's with a driving, hard rain. We didn't have good rain gear, and nearly froze before we got back to our cars. Several hikers have died on this mountain. You must be careful.

MOM TOLD US AT BREAKFAST THIS MORNING THAT A FRIEND JUST GOT GEOTHERMAL HEAT. WHAT'S THAT, GRAMPS?

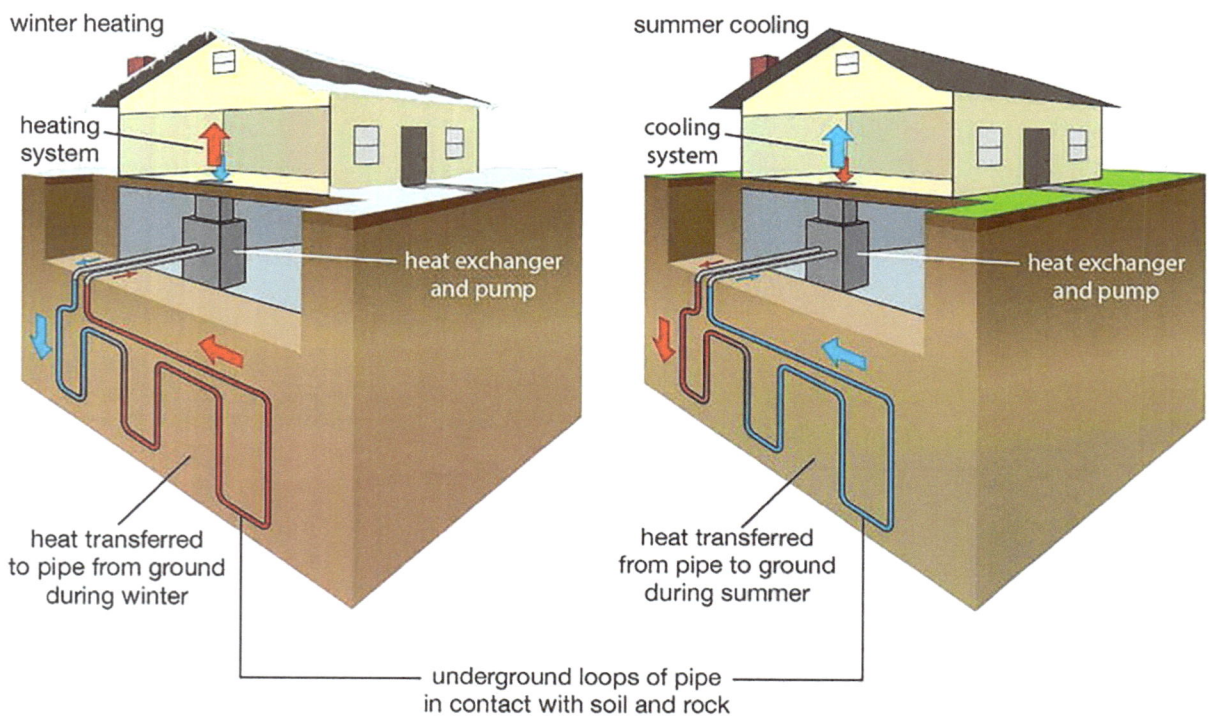

A geothermal heating system uses the fact that at 30 feet and lower under Earth's surface, temperatures remain about 55°F all year round.

CARLOS, A GEOTHERMAL HEATING SYSTEM takes advantage of this 55° F temperature by having a series of pipes buried deep in the ground near the home. The pipes are typically arranged in several loops and contain a mixture of water and antifreeze circulated by a pump to and from an indoor unit (see diagram).

In summer, the fluid in this loop moves heat from the house to deep in the ground where it is cooled to 55° F by the cool dirt and then returned to the home. A fan blows air over the cooler returning fluid to create cool air to circulate throughout the home to provide air-conditioning. A thermostat turns the fan off and on to maintain the desired temperature inside.

For heating, the same 55° F fluid in the pipes from outside now passes through a heat exchanger inside the home that uses a liquid refrigerant (typically R-410, often just called "Freon"). When this is sprayed onto the pipes coming from the ground it absorbs the 55° F heat and flashes instantly to a gas because Freon's boiling point is not 212° F like water, but -15° F. To the Freon, the 55° F water from the ground is very hot! However, the Freon gas is now still 55 degrees and cannot be used to heat the home to a toasty warm temperature. This is where we have to pay the utility company for electricity to run a compressor which squeezes this cold gas until it is very hot. Air from the home is now passed over pipes containing the hot gas warming it before it is sent throughout the home. During the summer, you get virtually free cooling, but during the winter we have to pay for electricity to run that compressor. Still geothermal is less expensive than heating the home with just electricity.

GRAMPA, I THOUGHT BENEDICT ARNOLD WAS A TRAITOR... YET I JUST READ THAT HE WAS A REAL MAINE HERO BEFORE THAT??

American colonists from Maine fighting British soldiers
Revolutionary War, Battle of Quebec, Winter, 1775

Benedict Arnold

Commemorative marker
in Eustis, Maine

BENEDICT ARNOLD IS A CONTROVERSIAL figure in American history, Rose. When his troops captured Fort Ticonderoga in May 1775, Arnold became one of George Washington's most trusted soldiers. Later that year Washington chose Arnold to lead a force of 1100 men north from Boston through what is now Maine to attack the British fort at Quebec in Canada.

The plan was to take flat wooden boats, called bateaux, up the Kennebec River, carry the boats to the Chaudière River and reach the Saint Lawrence River near Quebec. Maine did not exist yet as a state and was mostly wild, challenging territory. Bad winter weather, leaky bateaux, and the lack of good maps made it an extremely difficult journey. By the time Arnold reached Quebec, he had only half of his men left and most were sick and starving. He began an unsuccessful siege of Quebec and was later wounded during an assault. Upon his return to Massachusetts he was promoted to Brigadier General. The trail through Maine which Arnold covered is now called "The Arnold Trail to Canada." There is a marker at Eustis, Maine commemorating the colonists who made this difficult journey.

Three years later, now a Major General, Arnold was placed in charge of the critical American fort at West Point, New York. His wife, a close friend of the head of British espionage, is thought to have influenced him to plan to switch sides by handing over West Point to the British in September 1780 for a large sum of money. When his plans were discovered, Arnold escaped and joined the British, but his name is now synonymous with traitor. Arnold died in disgrace in England in 1801.

OUR BLACKFLIES HERE IN MAINE WERE REALLY ANNOYING EARLIER THIS YEAR, GRANDFATHER. WHERE ARE THEY THE REST OF THE YEAR?

Adult Black fly

Black fly larvae (stringy things attached to rocks) in fresh water (Photo courtesy of National Park Service)

OH, THEY'RE AROUND ALL YEAR, Jennifer. It's just that you can't see them except when they are flying around trying to bite us in early summer. When I was your age, we had only two types of black flies here in Maine, usually out biting from late May to early July. Now we have over 40 types, so it's possible to be annoyed for most of the summer – but not as much as during May and June "prime time."

The life cycle of these "bad girls" (the females are the only ones which bite humans and animals – the males eat only pollen) is short and glorious. Most blackfly species spend the winter in streams as larvae which have hatched from eggs laid in or near water. The larvae attach themselves to any underwater object and survive by breathing oxygen in the water through their skin. Because Maine has successfully cleaned up most of our streams and waterways, black flies have flourished due to increased amounts of oxygen in our clean waters. When spring comes, the flies transform into pupae and then ride an air bubble to the surface as an adult fly.

As I mentioned, it's the female which is looking for blood. Some bite the first mammal or bird that they find, while others are picky and want a particular meal, such as a dog or cow – or you! The only good news is that black flies here don't transmit diseases – just misery. Once they have blood, the females find a mate, lay eggs, and die – all in one or two days! Most initial bites on humans swell and are painful, but as you get more bites, our bodies seem to get used to it. I've found no insect repellant which works – just make sure you're covered up with clothing!

POPS, WHAT IS YOUR FAVORITE MAINE LIGHTHOUSE?

Rockland Harbor Breakwater Light

Portland Head Light
(courtesy of Christopher Larson)

THAT'S A TOUGH ONE TO answer, Chip. There are currently 57 active lighthouses on the coast of Maine, but my favorite is the Rockland Harbor Breakwater Light, probably because your grandmother and I have walked out the breakwater leading to it from the shore so many times.

The best place to learn about our lighthouses is the Maine Lighthouse Museum in Rockland where you can learn about how different types of lenses have been developed to shine light to aid in the safe navigation of ships at sea as they approach land. Ships see these lights, which have unique characteristics (for example, how often they flash) and draw a line on a chart (map) extending outward from the lighthouse's position. That way the ship knows it is somewhere on that line. If another light is available in that area, they draw a line from it – where the lines intersect tells you where the ship is located.

The oldest lighthouse in Maine is the Portland Head Light, which was built in 1791, not long after we became a nation. Like all the other operating lighthouses in Maine, its light is now automated. It also has a foghorn so ships can hear it during foggy conditions. How far you can see a lighthouse's light is determined by its height and type of light. The Portland light can be seen 28 miles at sea on a clear night. There are also 4 other lighthouses near Portland, so it's a good place to visit.

The first lighthouses used open flames from fires or candles and then switched to lamps burning whale oil. Now most use LED bulbs with sophisticated lenses – all controlled remotely.

GRANDPA, OUR TEACHER MENTIONED SOMETHING CALLED THE THOREAU-WABANAKI TRAIL. WHAT IS THIS?

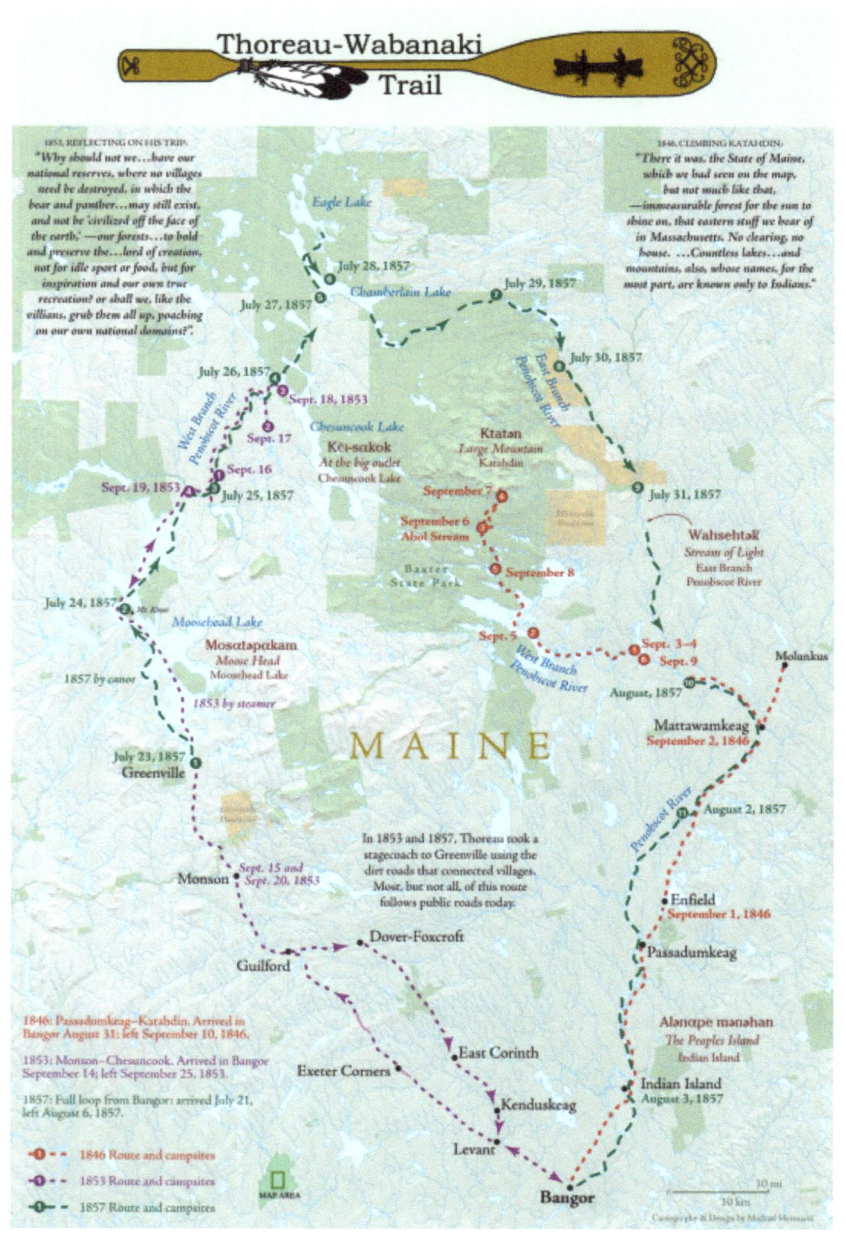

Ahmed, Henry David Thoreau was a famous American writer. He is known by many only for his book, "Walden," which is based on a two-year period in the 1840's when Thoreau lived by himself in a cabin on the edge of a pond in Massachusetts. This book gives his thoughts about "basic living" and what we can learn from a close relationship with nature.

But Thoreau was also close to nature in Maine. He made three trips here, all adventures in the deep woods of northern Maine. His first was in August 1846 when with friends he traveled in bateaux from Bangor up the Penobscot River to remote lakes. They then hiked on trails to reach Ktaadn (how Mount Katahdin was then spelled).

Seven years later Thoreau traveled by land to Greenville, at the southern tip of Moosehead Lake where he hired a Native American, Joe Attean, to be his guide on a trip by canoe to explore Chesuncook Lake in the far north.

Thoreau's third adventure in Maine was in 1857. This time he was accompanied by a member of the Wabanaki tribe, Joe Polis. After climbing Mount Kineo, they traveled via canoe and portages (carrying the canoe to the next water) in a long circular route through mostly uninhabited sections on the Kennebec, Allagash, and Penobscot rivers back to Bangor. Their route is now called the Thoreau-Wabanaki Trail. Each year a festival is held in Greenville to commemorate their experiences. I recommend you read Thoreau's writings about these Maine adventures in his book, "The Maine Woods."

GRANDDAD, I KEEP HEARING ABOUT "AQUACULTURE" IN MAINE. WHAT IS IT?

A fish farm near the Maine coast

Oysters

Atlantic Salmon

Kelp

KELLY, THE TERM "AQUACULTURE" SIMPLY means farming in water. Here in Maine it is a rapidly growing industry due to our lengthy coastline and having so many experienced watermen.

Many different creatures can be grown and harvested. For example, several types of shellfish (oysters, mussels, clams, and scallops) are grown. Oysters and scallops are typically raised in floating cages (see photo), while mussels are sometimes planted on the bottom of the sea. Fish, such as Atlantic salmon, are raised in pens enclosed by nets in the ocean, but also in tanks on land with seawater circulated in and out with pipes. Sometimes aquaculture companies raise fish and shellfish in a combined operation where nutrients from the fish stimulate growth for shellfish or plants which are being grown in the same area. This is done both in the ocean or in land tanks.

I mentioned plants because they are becoming an important part of the aquaculture business. There are several seaweeds which are grown, but the most important is kelp. It is a large, brown algae seaweed that prefers to grow in cold waters like we have in Maine. It's not exactly a plant, because it has no root. But like trees, it uses photosynthesis from the sun. Kelp grows naturally but is also farmed in Maine. It is processed for use in salad dressings, shampoos, toothpaste, and many other products. It can be eaten fresh, dried, or cooked – or even in a smoothie! Aquaculture here is often controversial due to environmental issues, such as wastewater discharge from these farms and oxygen depletion, but most can be resolved. Like all human activity, we need to balance the good and the bad.

GRAMPS, I HAVEN'T SEEN A MOOSE THIS YEAR. ARE THEY BECOMING ENDANGERED?

Bull Moose

Cow Moose with calf

No, Bobby, it's estimated that Maine has over 75,000 moose. They are not evenly distributed throughout our state because they prefer to live mostly in the deep woods of the northern part of Maine. You haven't seen one this year because you've been in the wrong place at the wrong time!

The moose population is closely monitored by the Department of Inland Fisheries and Wildlife using aerial surveys to ensure that we keep a stable number of moose – not too many, and not too few. If the numbers start to decline, they issue fewer hunting permits. In a recent year, Maine granted over 4000 permits allowing lucky recipients to hunt a moose. I say "lucky" because over 72,000 people applied for a permit.

The biggest problem for our moose now is not avoiding hunters, but a new threat called the "winter tick." In late summer their eggs hatch and the larvae latch onto a passing moose. These ticks stay on the moose throughout the winter feeding on the blood of the moose until they drop off and lay eggs for the next cycle. One moose can have over 150,000 ticks on it during the winter! This causes severe blood loss, and as the moose rubs against trees to try to get rid of the ticks, crucial fur is lost. Young moose are especially at risk; ticks are the main reason moose calves die. Several solutions have been tried, but none has been successful. The current plan is to increase the number of hunting permits to decrease the number of moose so that the ticks have fewer animals to infest and thus decrease the tick population. Some even proposed tick collars, but have you ever tried to catch a moose to put a collar on it???

POPPOP, WHO WERE THE FIRST PEOPLE TO LIVE HERE IN MAINE?

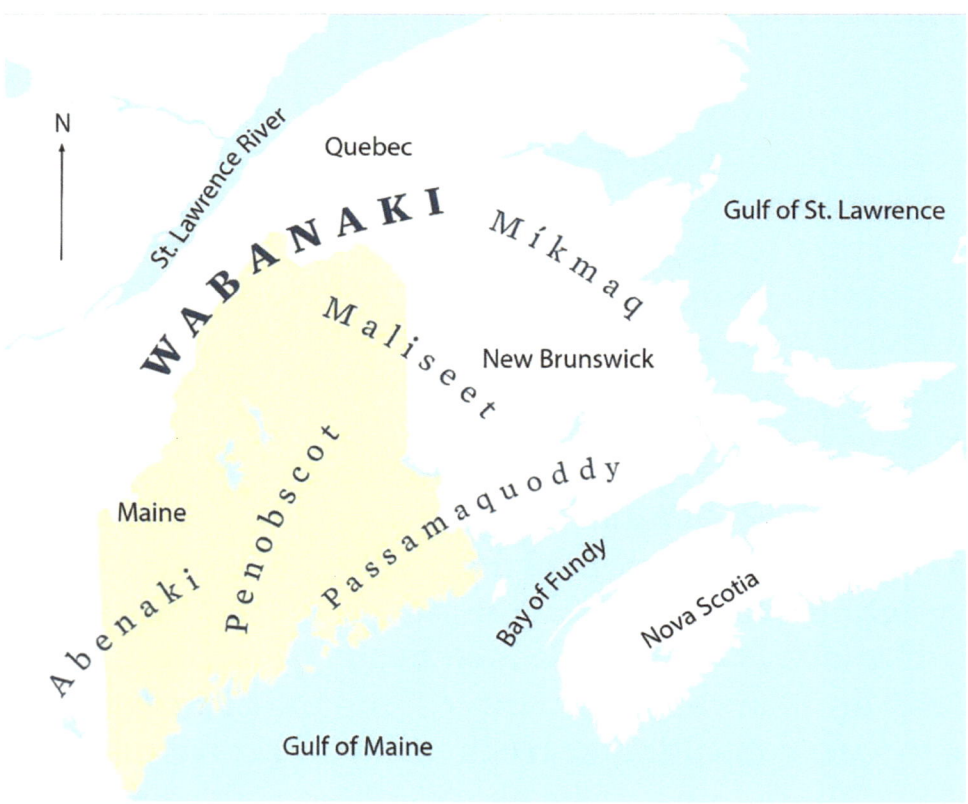

Indian Tribes in Northeast (Maine in yellow)

MARY, "OUR LAND" HAS SEEN a succession of different people living here throughout history. Much of what we know is based on archeology digs and dating of bones. Many of the different cultures resulted from climate and sea level changes. For example, many of the sites where earlier cultures lived are now submerged in the Gulf of Maine.

The first known humans living here nearly 12,000 years ago were "Paleoindians." They came east from what is now New York and used dugout canoes on our rivers and lakes. Their successors who lived here 3000-6000 years ago were called "Red Paint People," based on how they decorated their graves with red ochre (a natural reddish-brown pigment found in rocks and soil). They were hunters and boat builders and fished for swordfish. We don't know why they used this red paint, but it has been found in nearly every gravesite from this period.

The next culture, roughly 3000 years ago, has been called "the Susquehanna tradition." These people were hunters and had much in common with tribes as far south as the Carolinas.

Their successors (from 2800 to 500 years ago) were much the same as the Indian tribes (now referred to as "Native Americans") which were here when the Europeans arrived. They were the first to use birch bark canoes and to develop bows and arrows. They grew corn and beans in what is now the southwestern part of our state. Various tribes lived here as part of the "Wabanaki Confederacy" when the first Europeans arrived 500 years ago. You and I are truly newcomers!

GRAMPA, WHAT ARE "COLDWATER FISH"? I HEARD HANK'S DAD TALKING ABOUT CATCHING SOME LAST WEEK.

Brook Trout

Landlocked Salmon

Lake Trout (Togue)

Arctic Char

Splake

Cusk

WELL, MARK, THE NAME PRETTY much says it all. Coldwater fish are species which prefer to live in cold water as much as possible. Here in Maine we have 11 species of coldwater game fish, including four types of trout: Brook, Brown, Lake, and Rainbow. There are also Landlocked Salmon, Splake, Cusk, and Arctic Char, and a few others.

These fish prefer water temperatures below 65° F and spend summer days below the warmer surface water. Each species seems to have its favorite temperature, somewhere between cool and cold. Lake Trout (which are often called Togue) prefer very cold water year-round. In our local lake, using a fish finder, I have seen Togue spend most of the summer in deep holes 100 ft down where the water temperature is 50° F and below. During winter when lakes are covered with ice, the Togue come closer to the surface and are a prime target for ice fishing. In spring, when the ice cover is breaking up, all of these fish are hungry and can be found in shallow waters looking for smelts (a small fish) and insects.

Splake are an interesting fish because they are reared in hatcheries and are a hybrid cross between brook trout and lake trout. Like lake trout, they go deep in the summer, but most anglers contend that they are easier to catch than the others, especially during the winter months.

All of these coldwater fish are excellent to eat and are prized by most fishermen, including me!

BABA, DO BEARS HERE IN MAINE REALLY SLEEP ALL WINTER LONG?

Tranquilized mother bear with two cubs (ears tagged)

Biologist David Pert trying to exit a bear den after inspecting condition of bear family inside (Photo credits: Carl D. Walsh and NewEngland.com)

BEARS ARE USUALLY SAID TO "hibernate" during the winter in a low-energy state to survive cold temperatures and the lack of food supplies. Actually, Noel, our black bears are in a lighter-sleep state called "torpor." In this condition, breathing and heart rates decrease dramatically from 55 beats per minute to 9. Their body temperature decreases – all of these traits allow most bears to sleep more than 100 days without eating or drinking – or even pooping or peeing. Bears develop a "fecal plug" of undigested materials in their intestines which blocks all poop. Their urine is re-absorbed in their bladder and used as needed electrolytes. But a female bear which is pregnant will wake to give birth. Then the baby bear(s) are on their own and must crawl to their mommy's teats to feed on milk throughout the winter. The mother bear goes back to sleep.

To get ready for a long winter, bears will eat heavily in the fall to build up fat reserves for their lengthy sleep. Maine black bears will be in this state of torpor from 3-7 months, depending on the weather. Bears look for natural shelters, such as caves or thickets or hollow trees in which to sleep. Occasionally during the winter, bears will wake up for short periods and even go outside their dens before returning.

Maine biologists specializing in bear behavior will often enter a bear den with a tranquilizer gun to temporarily sedate the bear to check its health, examine and tag any babies, and keep track of the bear population. We currently have around 35,000 black bears in Maine. They are an important part of our ecosystem. Still, I am not volunteering to crawl into a bear den. NO WAY!

POPS, I HEARD ABOUT SOME 12-YEAR OLD KID WHO WAS LOST A LONG TIME AGO ON KATAHDIN FOR OVER A WEEK AND LIVED. IS THIS TRUE?

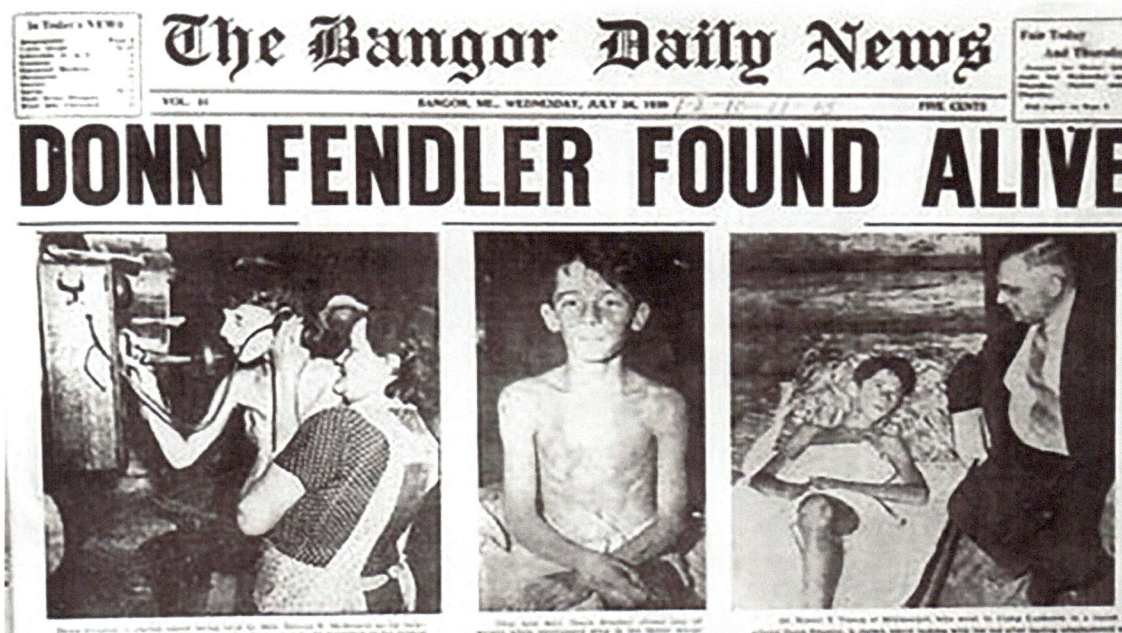

(Left) Donn Fendler as Boy Scout

(Right) Donn Fendler as Army Officer

WHAT YOU HEARD, ROBIN, IS definitely true. A young Boy Scout from New York, named Donn Fendler, was hiking on Katahdin with friends in July 1939 when he became separated and lost in the fog. Local mill workers raced to the scene to search for the boy. Soon family members and others, including a New York police unit with bloodhounds, joined the effort to find Donn.

The story swept the nation in newspapers and radios. Mothers all over the country sent telegrams to his grieving mother with prayers. Even the Governor of Maine and President Franklin Roosevelt offered support. As day after day passed with no sign of Donn, alive or dead, people began to give up hope. Search planes could not find him. How could a city kid with no food or appropriate clothing possibly survive the harsh challenges of this mountain?

But Donn kept up hope and battled the elements, insects, wildlife, and lack of food. He was not on a trail but kept stumbling down the mountain, wandering over 80 miles. Finally, after 8 days Donn walked into a camp where he was treated by an elderly couple. They then took him by canoe to a small town, Grindstone, where he was transported by ambulance to a hospital in Bangor. Amazingly, Donn suffered no serious injuries and became a national hero. He attributed his survival to a strong will to live...and luck.

Donn returned to school, served in the Navy during WW II and then in the Army for 28 years. He wrote a best-selling book, "Lost on a Mountain in Maine," about his adventure on Katahdin.

GRANDPA, DO WE HAVE ANY FIRE TOWERS STILL IN USE HERE IN MAINE?

Fire Tower on Fire Tower on Spencer Mountain (no longer active)

Active Fire Tower on Mount Hope

Fire Tower on Bald Mountain (Removed in 2009)

Y ES, SHARRY, WE HAVE TWO left. Both are in York County – one on Mount Hope, the other on Ossipee Hill. Both towers are now manned by volunteers. At one time, we had 144 towers spread throughout the woods of Maine. Most have been torn down, but there are still about 50 standing.

In 1891, Maine state legislators saw the need to try to protect our forests from wild fires and established a State Forest Commission. Fires have always been the greatest threat to our forests; in 1903 alone, over 200,000 acres were burned in fires. Obviously, you can't put out a fire until you know where it is, so early detection is a big help. Towers, manned by rangers, were built so that observers could report the location of a fire quickly. The first one was built in 1904 by lumber companies on one of the mountains near Greenville.

Many other fire towers were soon added on other mountains. They were manned from spring to late fall (winter snowfalls greatly lessened the chances of fires). Each of these early towers was constructed of wood and equipped with telephones powered by batteries and hand cranks. Later, many of these towers were torn down and replaced with steel structures. The fire wardens used binoculars to sight fires and often lived in nearby cabins, taking turns for lookout duty. How far the wardens could see depended on the height of the tower and the daily visibility. Airplanes, satellites, and drones are now our eyes to detect forest fires.

On our next hike to Kineo let's climb the old fire tower there!

GRAMPS, I KEEP HEARING THAT SEVERAL CITIES HERE IN MAINE WERE "MILL TOWNS." WHAT WAS THAT?

Young Mill Worker

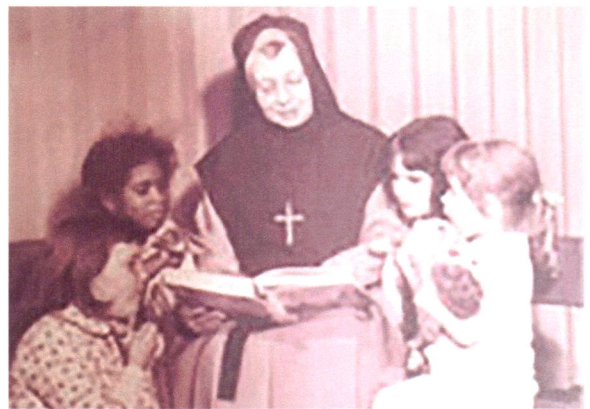

A "Grey Nun" at Lewiston orphanage

Old mill buildings in Biddeford

Old Bates mill in Lewiston

Mill towns, Carmen, are an important part of Maine history. These were towns where most of the opportunities to work were only in large manufacturing companies called mills. Some made paper from trees, others made textiles from cotton and wool, a few ground grain. Our many rivers provided the energy to turn water wheels attached to gears to power ingenious, complicated machinery to create clothing, lumber, and food.

Entire towns grew around these mills which employed thousands of workers. For example, by the 1850's the mills in Biddeford had 3500 employees creating millions of yards of cotton fabric which was sold throughout the world – even to China.

During the early 1800's most of the workers were young farm girls who flocked to mill towns for work and independence. Many of the jobs were later taken over by immigrants, mostly French Canadians coming south seeking work. Lewiston, known as "Little Canada," had so many French Canadian children that "Grey Nuns" (called that because of their grey clothing) were recruited from Canada in 1878 to teach French and to establish a hospital and orphanage.

It is difficult today to imagine most citizens in any Maine city being dependent on one or two companies, but that is what life in a mill town was like. The mills dominated most aspects of life in the town. When alternate sources of energy became available, many of the mills moved to southern states to be closer to where the cotton was grown. It was the end of an era in Maine, but many of the original buildings are still standing.

GRANDFATHER, DID MAINE COON CATS REALLY ORIGINATE IN MAINE?

DOYLE, NOT ONLY IS THE Maine Coon Cat THE official cat of Maine, it's also the most registered cat breed in the U.S. They're a lot of myths circulating about how these cats first reached Maine. One of my favorites involves the Queen of France, Marie Antoinette (the one who said "Let them eat cake" when she was told that the poor had no bread to eat). When she was trying to escape France, the story goes, she loaded her favorite possessions, including six Turkish Angora cats, onto a ship. She never made it to the U.S., but her cats did. All six reached Wiscasset where they were bred with local cats and became called the Coon Cat. Few believe this myth, but it's a good tale.

Most now agree that because it is a long-haired cat, the Coon descended from Norwegian cats brought here by either Vikings or other settlers. What is certain is that people were writing about Coon Cats just prior to our Civil War in the 1860's. The Skowhegan Fair even held a "Maine State Champion Coon Cat" contest around 1870. By 1895 a Maine Coon won the "Best in Show" at the first North American Cat Show in New York City. For some reason, possibly due to other similar breeds of cats becoming available, the Coon declined dramatically in popularity and was nearly extinct by 1950. But the Central Maine Cat Club kept the breed alive and soon Maine Coon Cats regained popularity nationally.

The Coon Cat's fur is soft and silky (and water-resistant) and requires less grooming than other long-haired cats. It is ideal for cold climates, like ours. It's a BIG cat with a long tail which almost looks like a raccoon's. Most owners love their Coon Cats!

AUTHOR'S NOTE

To me, Maine is a very special place. I arrived here later in life when my wife recommended that we kayak its lakes and to visit Lewiston, where she attended high school. Over the following decade, we enjoyed so many memorable days kayaking Maine lakes and ponds and hiking Katahdin twice.

During one of our visits, we fell in love with the Moosehead Lake region and ultimately bought a small, but comfortable, camp outside Greenville. Here I have been struck by the warm friendship of so many Mainers. It's as if we have lived here all our lives.

My hope is that not only Maine children, but others everywhere who love nature and history, will find the back and forth stories between grandchildren and their grandfathers in this book to be both interesting and enjoyable.

Author outside Monson on the 100 Mile Wilderness Section of the Appalachian Trail

www.ingramcontent.com/pod-product-compliance
Lightning Source LLC
Chambersburg PA
CBHW041103070526
44583CB00002B/42